Ancient Egypt

sacred symbols

Ancient Egypt

Thames & Hudson

A World of Symbols

For the Ancient Egyptians the whole world, as they saw it, was represented symbolically. From the sun and the Nile, which gave them food and sustenance, to the animal kingdom, wild and domestic, everything was imbued with hidden meaning. Even their architecture, and especially

that associated with funerary rites, was full of
complex meaning and significance. At its deepest
level, symbolism was the means by which the
Egyptians expressed their speculations about the
nature of life itself – the creation, the after-life and
the struggle between good and evil.

A gift from the gods

the written language of the Ancient Egyptians was truly symbolic and very much associated with the gods themselves. Just how closely the image and the act of writing itself were connected is demonstrated by there being a single word for 'drawing' and 'writing'. Truly symbolic were the hieroglyphic signs for the gods; thus, Horus was represented by a falcon, Isis by a throne, Seth by a desert animal with an arrow-like tail and Anubis by a jackal. And much of the rest of the language was symbolic — 'to walk' was signified by two legs; 'house' was represented by a rectangle with an opening in its lower part.

The representations of the god Thoth were many – ibis-headed, baboon, or god of the moon. Of great importance to the Egyptians was his role as god of writing and patron of scribes, since language was considered to be a gift direct from the gods. For this reason, the god-baboon is often represented watching over a crouching, subservient scribe.

CHAOS AND COSMOS

Symbols and Gods of Creation and the Life-Force

the Ancient Egyptian religious texts offer several explanations of the creation, usually differing according to their place of origin. One strong tradition told of the emergence of a mound from the watery chaos. Another version of this tradition included a lotus floating upon the primeval waters and then opening to reveal the new-born sun. Creation by utterance was another common tradition; at Memphis the creator god Ptah is supposed to have initiated the cosmos by simply speaking the thought.

nut

Called 'the female pig who eats her piglets', mother
of all the heavenly bodies which entered her mouth
and emerged again from her womb, the sky goddess
Nut is usually represented arching over Shu, her
father, god of air, and Geb, her husband and brother,
god of the earth, who help to support her (overleaf).
As the goddess of the cyclical working of the cosmos,
Nut was also intimately connected to the idea of
resurrection. The sarcophagus and tomb chamber were
often decorated with stars and the goddess's image.

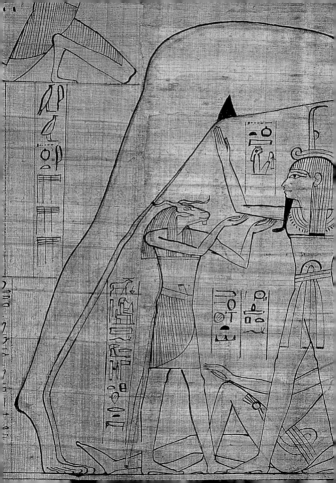

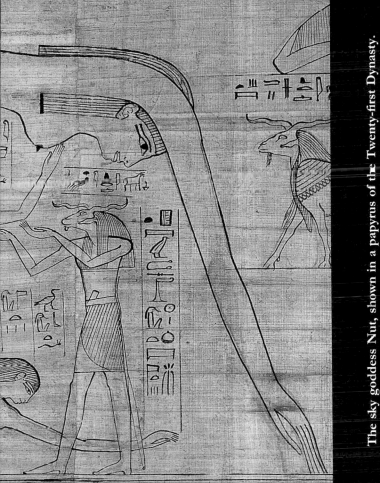

The sky goddess Nut, shown in a papyrus of the Twenty-first Dynasty.

tefnut

One of the oldest Egyptian creation myths
visualized the earth as a mound rising from
the watery chaos of Nun. On the mound was the
self-created Atum, who then created Shu, god of air,
and Tefnut, goddess of moisture, thus releasing
duality into the world and the beginning of the
sexual cycle. When Atum was assimilated into Re,
Tefnut and her brother became the children of the
sun god. In this papyrus of the Nineteenth Dynasty
Tefnut is represented with an ankh in the role of one
of the Great Ennead judges of the Underworld.

Opposite Tefnut, goddess
of life-giving dew,
Papyrus of Hunefer,
Nineteenth Dynasty.

apis bull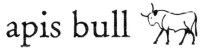

as one of the strongest pro-life, procreative symbols of Ancient Egypt, the bull could represent the composite god of creation, the primeval water or even the inundation of the Nile. This identification with the creative life-force also meant that the bull was identified with the Egyptian king and a number of New Kingdom monarchs were described as 'mighty bull' or 'bull of Horus'.

Opposite Twentieth Dynasty coffin painting showing the bull as god of creation and rebirth.

Right Bronze of Apis bull, Late Period.

Hail to you, you who shine in your disc, a living soul who goes up from the horizon... I know the names of the seven cows and their bull who give bread and beer, who are beneficial to souls.

The Egyptian Book of the Dead, Spell 148

sun and moon

The passage of the sun through the vault of the heavens, represented by the goddess Nut; she touches the western and eastern horizons with her hands and feet. Nut was the deity for all heavenly bodies and mother of the sun god Re, whom she swallowed in the evening and regurgitated in the morning, thus associating herself with the symbolism of resurrection. In Heliopolitan theology she was the daughter of Shu, the air god, and sister of Geb, the earth god. The moon was the 'sun shining at night', the left eye of the sky god. It was usually represented in the form of a disc resting on a crescent, worn as a head-dress by the moon god Khons.

Opposite A tomb-ceiling painting of the sun's night-time journey through the body of Nut, Twentieth Dynasty.

Figure of Iah, 'the moon' in human form, with crescent moon and disc, Late Period.

A limestone carving of the royal family, Eighteenth Dynasty.

O sun-disc, Lord of the sunbeams, who shines forth from the horizon every day: may you shine in the face of the deceased, for he worships you in the morning, he propitiates you in the evening. May he moor in the Night-bark, may he mix with the Unwearying Stars in the sky.
The Egyptian Book of the Dead, Spell 15

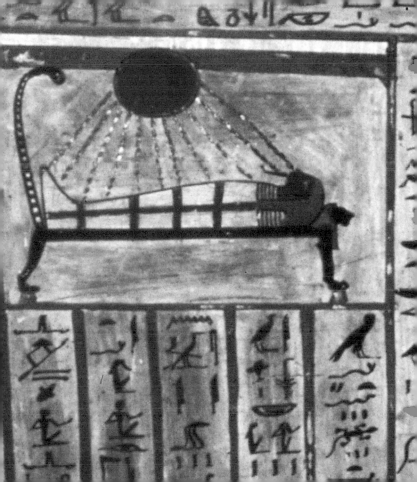

osiris

'The eternally good king' or 'the perfect one' under his received name of Wennefer, Osiris was at the centre of the most extensive symbolism of Ancient Egypt. He began as a fertility god with a special association with corn and with the life-giving waters of the Nile, called the 'efflux of Osiris'. After receiving the rulership of the earth from his father Geb, Osiris introduced vine-growing and agriculture to the country. All this engaged the envy of his brother Seth who caused him to be drowned in the Nile, symbolizing the flooding of the land and the new harvest.

Hail to you, Osiris Wennefer, the vindicated, the son of Nut; King in the Thinite nome; Foremost of the Westerners; Lord of Abydos; Lord of Power, greatly majestic...

The Egyptian Book of the Dead, Spell 128

Opposite Tutankhamun, represented as Osiris, undergoes the ritual of the opening of the mouth by King Ay, in a painting from his own tomb.

osiris and horus

Divine mourners Isis and Nephthyx protect the *djed*-
column, symbol of Osiris, with their wings.

The falcon, king of the air, was the creature of Horus and symbol of divine kingship. Here, this expression of domination and triumph surmounts the **djed** pillar, ancient fetish and feature of rustic fertility rites. Given its architectural character, the pillar took on associations of stability and, most interesting, became a symbol for Osiris at the beginning of the New Kingdom, when it was seen to represent the god's backbone. The raising of the pillar represented the victory of Osiris over Seth.

Right Djed-column, surmounted by the falcon with the sun disc.

maat

Without this goddess, the whole process of
creation and constant renewal would have
been meaningless. She symbolizes the laws of
existence – law, truth and the world order;
judges were thought of as the priests of Maat.
The cyclical nature of life would have been
impossible without her: she was food and
drink to Re, her father, the sun god. She
was represented wearing an ostrich feather,
which came to be a symbol of truth.

Opposite Maat with
her ostrich feather
in her head-band,
symbol of truth.

the tree of life

the tree, especially date palm and sycamore, was indeed the symbol of life for the Ancient Egyptians, since it grew where there was life-giving water. Sycamores had particular significance, and two special ones were supposed to stand at the eastern gate of heaven from which Re emerged each day. There was widespread worship of the tree in the Nile valley; several deities were believed to have been born from trees – Horus from the

Spell for knowing the Soul of Easterners

I know those two trees of turquoise between which **Re** goes forth, which have grown up at the Supports of Shu at that gate of the Lord of East where **Re** goes forth.

The Egyptian Book of the Dead, Spell 109

acacia, Re from the sycamore and Wepwawet from the tamarisk. Images of female tree spirits, representing the sky goddesses Nut and Hathor, abound; the deities give water and fruit to the soul of the deceased which is represented in bird form.

Opposite The goddess Isis from a tomb painting of Thutmosis III.

the waters of life

It is hardly surprising that water in Ancient Egypt was the subject of extensive symbolism; it was, after all, the very life source of the country. It was the primeval matter from which all things had come; it provided purification; it was a symbol of reproduction. As god of vegetation, Osiris was also lord of the waters of the Nile, linking him to the inundation which was vital to the continuation of cultivation and the fertility of the land, separately represented by Isis.

Opposite The deceased drinking the waters in the shade of a palm, Twentieth Dynasty.

Spell for drinking water in the realm of the dead

May the great water be opened for Osiris, may the cool water of Thoth and the water of Hapi be thrown open for the Lord of the Horizon in this my name of Pedsu. May I be granted power over the waters like the limbs of Seth, for I am he who crosses the sky, I am the Lion of Re, I am the Slayer who eats the foreleg, the leg of beef is extended to me, the pools of the Field of Rushes serve me, limitless eternity is given to me, for I am he who inherited eternity to whom everlasting life was given.

The Egyptian Book of the Dead, Spell 62

the river of life

the Nile, personified here as a man, bears the palm-rib, which is also the hieroglyph for 'year', symbolizing the annual flooding of the river (opposite).

Although fish were generally thought unclean, the bulti fish was taken as a potent symbol of rebirth, a reference to the incubation and hatching of eggs in its mouth.

the life-force

the creative force and power of life found expression
at the personal, individual level in the **ka**.
Symbolized by two upraised arms, the **ka** was a
person's double, embodying intellectual and spiritual
power. The defensive posture of the arms is designed
to ward off evil forces which may attack the life-spirit
of the wearer. Each person was born with his or her
ka, which was a constant companion through life
and lived on after death, returning to its divine
origin. However, the **ka** did need sustenance, and
food itself was regarded as having its own **ka**. In its
earliest form the **ka** represented male potency and
only later came to have its all-embracing significance.

King Hor wearing the *ka*
head-dress, Thirteenth
Dynasty.

POWER AND POTENCY

Symbols of Status and Good Fortune

Sphinx and Pyramid, two of
the strongest symbols of
status and power in Ancient
Egyptian thought.

t he power and standing of gods and kings was expressed through an elaborate system of personal symbols, from head-dress to amulet. The greatest symbolic embodiment of regal power was the Sphinx, firm but benevolent.

crown

the crown of the Egyptian king was looked upon as a source of nourishment whereby its power was transferred to the ruler. Since Egypt was a country of 'two lands' the kings wore the 'Double Crown', the pschent, combining the mitre form of the White Crown of Upper Egypt with the Red Crown of Lower Egypt. According to period the crowns took different forms, from the 'double-feathers' crown of two upright ostrich plumes to the blue Khepresh crown with gold ornamentation. The royal crowns were also seen as the eye of the sun god or as a flame around the king.

Opposite Head-dress of gold with vulture and cobra: Tutankhamun in the form of Osiris.

head-dress

The close association of Egyptian deities and animals is constantly expressed in the animal-headed figures in Egyptian art. Power is conferred by the head-dress and its form indicates the status of the wearer. Symbol of evil among the dwellers of the Nile delta was Seth, a human figure with a head-dress of an indeterminate species, part antelope, part ant-eater.

'He whose hinder-parts are extended' is the name of the keeper of the second gate; 'Shifting of face' is the name of him who guards it; 'Burner' is the name of him who makes report in it.

The Egyptian Book of the Dead, Spell 144.

Opposite Animal-headed figures in a tomb-painting of the Second Gate of the Underworld.

Above Statuette of the Seth animal, Twenty-second Dynasty.

vulture head-dress

When the Egyptian king went into battle he was protected by a vulture with a white head-dress. His own head-cloth was a symbol of the Upper Egyptian national goddess Nekhbet, who was also characterized by her wearing of a vulture head-dress. The vulture was, surprisingly, thought to play a protective role in the land of the dead. In the Late Period the bird came to embody the female principle, as opposed to the beetle, which was the embodiment of the male principle. As the heraldic animal of Upper Egypt and of the goddess Nekhbet, the vulture became an especially potent royal symbol and was often represented in royal graves. It was also the sacred animal of the goddess Mut, worshipped at Thebes.

Opposite Queen Nefertari wearing the vulture head-dress, symbol of protection.

ankh

The original significance of this mysterious Egyptian symbol is not clear. It has been suggested that its shape has sexual connotations, although there is support for the theory that it represents a simple sandal strap. Symbol of life and irresistible strength, representative of the life-giving attributes of air and water, the **ankh** was given by the gods to the king and is usually shown in the hands of some deity or its associated animal. This was one of the most powerful of all Egyptian amulets and retained its influence throughout Ancient Egyptian history, eventually entering Christian iconography during the Coptic period.

A gilded wooden mirror box in the *ankh* form.

Opposite The goddess Hathor with the *ankh* in the form of Osiris, Thebes, Twentieth Dynasty.

shen ring

the perfection of the shen ring amulet, without beginning or end, made it a very obvious symbol of eternity. Its round form also associated it with the disc of the sun and it was often depicted being held by animals and birds, such as the falcon, with strong solar connections. 'Magic' rings were very popular and were believed to give protection from various illnesses.

Spell for a knot-amulet of red jasper

You have your blood, O Isis; you have your power, O Isis; you have your magic, O Isis. The amulet is a protection for this Great One which will drive away whoever would commit a crime against him.

The Egyptian Book of the Dead, Spell 156

Opposite 'The goddess Isis, hands stretched over a shen ring, symbolizing eternity, Eighteenth Dynasty.

eye

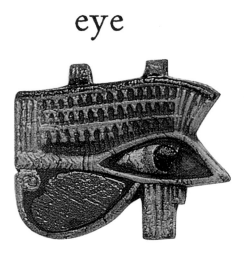

An eye amulet – symbolic jewellery for personal
protection.

One of the most important symbols of the
Ancient Egyptians, the eye was connected by
its round form with the sun.

The *wedjit* eye in this piece of jewellery was strongly associated with healing and protection. It was thought to protect the mummy's health and give the body new vitality.

Eyes watch over a falcon-headed god, forming a
protective shield.

the eyes of horus

The right eye of the falcon god Horus was known as the 'Eye of Re', the eye of the sun god; the left eye (the 'Eye of Horus') was regarded as the symbol of the moon. Of Horus it was written, 'When he opens his eyes he fills the universe with light but when he shuts them darkness comes into being'. The sacred eye symbol was undoubtedly a sign of protection; it appeared in countless articles of jewellery, especially amulets, and two eyes were often painted on the left side of coffins to enable the deceased to see the way ahead.

Spell for bringing a Sacred Eye by the deceased

Thoth has fetched the Sacred Eye, having pacified the Eye after Re had sent it away. It was very angry, but Thoth pacified it from anger after it had been far away. If I be hale, it will be hale, and the deceased will be hale.

The Egyptian Book of the Dead, Spell 167

BESTIARY AND BELIEF

Symbols from Nature

t he natural world and its parts – animals, birds, flowers – were seen by the Ancient Egyptians to symbolize much greater natural phenomena. The scarab rolling its ball of dung was the sun-god rolling the sun's orb across the sky. In one version of the cosmos, the wings of a falcon were seen as the broad sweep of the heavens, the speckled underside of the feathers representing the sky above.

Opposite A sa-ta snake walking on human legs from the Book of the Dead, a symbol of mystery and life creation.

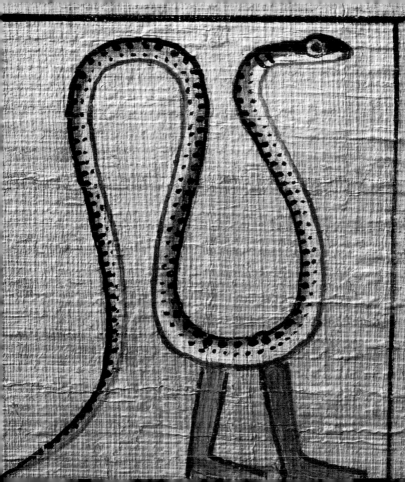

baboon

Faïence figure of a baboon clutching the eye symbol.

Closely associated with Thoth, the god of writing, the baboon is often represented in Egyptian art in the same context as scribes. Such figures often bear the lunar crescent and the solar disc on their heads: Thoth had originally been a moon god and it was believed that the cries uttered by baboons in the morning were a welcome to the early sun. The chief cult centre of Thoth was at Hermopolis where he took on the form of the baboon after merging with a deity of the region.

I am Thoth the skilled scribe whose hands are pure, a possessor of purity, who drives away evil, who writes what is true, who detests falsehood, whose pen defends the Lord of All; master of laws who interprets writings, whose words establish the Two Lands.

The Egyptian Book of the Dead, Spell 182

cat

the image of the cat in the earliest Egyptian symbolism was probably derived from the jungle cat which lived in the Nile delta. In the New Kingdom the male cat was seen as an incarnation of the sun god and the she-cat as the solar eye. The domestic cat was the sacred animal of the goddess Bastet, usually depicted as a woman with the head of a cat.

A bronze figure of a cat, representing the goddess Bastet, Late Period.

Cats sacred to the
goddess Bastet
were mummified
when they died.

scarab

Detail of a scarab bracelet from the tomb of Tutankhamun, Thebes.

Symbol of self-creation, the scarab was believed to come directly into being from the balls of animal dung which it used to protect its eggs and larva. Associated with the sun and therefore with life-giving warmth and light, pottery models of the scarab were often placed in tombs as a symbol of the renewal of life. Again, in its solar role, the scarab represented the morning sun in its god-form of Khepri. In his beetle form the god rose as the morning sun from the eastern horizon. A strong life god, Khepri also symbolized resurrection.

I have flown up like the primeval ones, I have become khepri, I have grown as a plant, I have clad myself as a tortoise, I am the essence of every god ....
The Egyptian Book of the Dead, Spell 83

falcon

Gold falcon ornament clutching shen rings and ankhs.

So many Egyptian deities were associated with the falcon that the image of the bird came to be virtually synonymous with 'god'. Its regal flight and aggressive qualities made it a natural symbol for Horus, king of the gods, and for divine kingship in general. Other falcon gods included Month, the god of war, Re, the sun god, and Sokar, the god of mortuaries. The original image of Horus was of a falcon protecting the heavens and earth with outstretched wings.

Right Bronze figure of the falcon god Horus, Twenty-sixth Dynasty.

ibis

The sacred ibis enjoyed very special status as the incarnation of Thoth, lord of the moon and the protector of scribes. Thoth's main cult centre at Hermopolis was also the burial ground for thousands of mummified ibises. The crested ibis was also used as a symbol for 'transfiguration'.

In Spell 183 of The Egyptian Book of the Dead Thoth, with an ibis head, offers symbols, including the ankh, to Osiris for 'all life and dominion' (opposite).

Ibis coffin in gilded wood, silver and gold, Macedonian/Ptolemaic Period.

vulture

Armlet of Queen Ah-hotpe in the form of a vulture, Western Thebes.

cobra

the cobra was seen principally as a solar symbol, with close connections to many deities. One of the most notable was the goddess Wadjet of the city of Buto and, through her, the cobra came to be an emblem of Lower Egypt.

Spell for being transformed into a snake

I am a long-lived snake; I pass the night and am reborn every day. I am a snake which is in the limits of the earth; I pass the night and am reborn, renewed and rejuvenated every day.

The Egyptian Book of the Dead, Spell 87

Rising cobra wearing the Red Crown, made from sheet gold, Late Period.

crocodile

the crocodile was seen as an agent of disorder and was associated with the evil god Seth. So strong was crocodile imagery in Egyptian symbolic thought, that The Book of the Dead contains a number

Get back you crocodile of the East who lives on those who are mutilated.
Detestation of you is in my belly, and I have gone away, for I am Osiris.
The Egyptian Book of the Dead, Spell 32

*of recipes for repelling the reptiles. Yet, since it had emerged from
the waters like the sun god, the crocodile also had more positive
connotations as a force for life and renewal.*

Spell for being transformed into a lotus
I am this pure lotus which went forth from the sunshine, which
is at the nose of Re; I have descended so that I may seek it for
Horus, for I am the pure one who issued from the fen.
The Egyptian Book of the Dead, Spell 81A

lotus

As the sun rises, in the morning, in the most, the waterlily, the lotus, opens itself to greet the renewal of light. So, the flower became the symbol of the re-emerging sun after the night and therefore associated with the sun god Re who is portrayed in The Book of the Dead *as a golden youth rising from the lotus. Thus the flower, especially the blue lotus, also came to symbolize rebirth. The portrait head of Tutankhamun (opposite) is shown rising from a blue lotus, signifying his resurrection.*

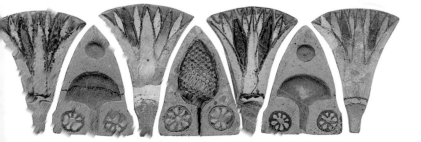

THE AFTERLIFE

Symbols for the Dead

The great pyramids
of Giza, Fourth
Dynasty.

all Ancient Egyptian architecture – especially shrines and burial places had symbolic meaning. The pyramid, which may also have symbolized the mound of creation rising from the primeval waters, was intimately associated with the sun.

anubis dog

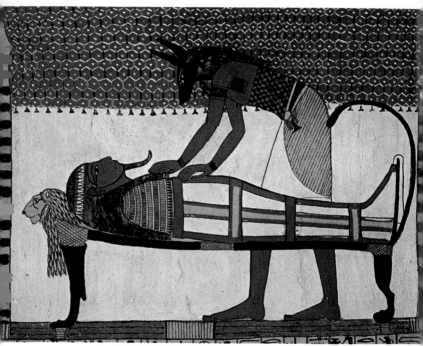

Anubis embalms the nobleman Sennedjem, Nineteenth Dynasty.

U*sually represented in canine form —dog or jackal — Anubis was the principal god of the dead before Osiris. He was closely associated with the necropolis and known as 'God of the Hallowed Land'. Representations of Anubis were placed in the tomb to guard the mummification chamber and frighten away evil.*

Spell for breathing air and having power over water in the realm of the dead

I shall cross to the Mansion of Him who finds faces; 'Collector of soul' is the name of the ferryman... you shall give me a jug of milk, a shens-loaf, a persen-loaf, a jug of beer and a portion of meat in the Mansions of Anubis

The Egyptian Book of the Dead, Spell 58

Wood figure of Anubis, god of the dead, coated with stucco and painted, Late Period.

door/stairs

the symbolism of the door was dual – it could represent
closure or entry and is seen with both such meanings
in Ancient Egyptian art. In tombs and shrines doors
would be decorated with various symbols, usually
signifying the transition from one state to the next -- into
heaven or into the deepest part of the underworld.
When the doors of tombs are depicted as open, it was
supposed that the spirit of the deceased, symbolically, had
free access to the buried body and that the **ka** could
come and go at will. As symbols of transition, ascension
and descent, staircases and ladders were as potent as
doorways. Every Egyptian tomb incorporated a stairway
which led down into the inner chamber.

Opposite Interior of
the chapel of a
nobleman, Sixth
Dynasty.

shrine

*In its Upper Egyptian form, the **Per-wer** or **Kar**,
the shrine came to symbolize the whole of the
southern region. Such shrines housed the image of
the appropriate god and were usually kept in a
separate room at the rear of the god's house, from
which it might be taken for religious processions or
rituals. The Lower Egyptian shrine, the **Per-nu**,
had a domed roof and high side posts, in contrast to
the sloping roof and prominent cornice of the **Per-
wer**. In* The Book of Gates *a row of twelve
Per-nu shrines is shown with doors open displaying
the gods inside – while a huge serpent lies along the
whole length as a symbol of protection.*

Shrine from the tomb of
Tutankhamun in the Upper
Egyptian form, Eighteenth
Dynasty.

ba

A human-headed *ba* in
glass and cornelian.

*Often inadequately translated as 'soul' the **ba** should really
be more properly thought of as a psychic force. First ascribed
to gods, then later applied to all people, the **ba** was the
spiritual aspect of the human being which survived death.*

O you who cause the perfected souls to draw to the
House of Osiris, may you cause the excellent soul of the
deceased to draw near with you to the House of Osiris.
May he hear as you hear, may he see as you see, may he
stand as you stand, may he sit as you sit.

Opposite The *ba* was often
shown in bird-form in tomb
paintings.

Chronological Table of Ancient Egypt

Late Predynastic Period (*c.* 3000 BC)

Early Dynastic Period (2920-2649)

Dynasty 1	2920-2770
Dynasty 2	2770-2649

Old Kingdom (2649-2150)

Dynasty 3	2649-2575
Dynasty 4	2575-2465
Dynasty 5	2465-2323
Dynasty 6	2323-2150

First Intermediate Period (2150-2040)

Dynasty 7	2150-2134
Dynasty 8	2150-2134
Dynasty 9	2134-2040
Dynasty 10	2134-2040

Middle Kingdom (2040-1991)

Dynasty 11	2040-1991
Dynasty 12	1991-1783
Dynasty 13	1783-1640

Second Intermediate Period (1640-1550)

Dynasty 14-17	1640-1550

New Kingdom (1550-1070)

Dynasty 18 1550-1307
Dynasty 19 1307-1196
Dynasty 20 1307-1070

Third Intermediate Period (1070-712)

Dynasty 21 1070-945
Dynasty 22 945-712
Dynasty 23 828-712
Dynasty 24 724-712

Late Period (712-332)

Dynasty 25 . . . . 712-657 (Kushite)
Dynasty 26 . . . . 664-525 (Saite)
Dynasty 27 525-404
Dynasty 28 404-399
Dynasty 29 399-380
Dynasty 30 380-343
Dynasty 31 . . . . 343-332 (Persian)

Greco-Roman Period (332 BC-AD 395)

Macedonian Dynasty . . 332-304
Ptolemaic Dynasty 304-30
Roman Emperors . . . . 30 BC-AD 395

Sources of Illustrations and Quotations

The Walters Art Gallery, Baltimore 52; Staatliche Museen Berlin, Bildarchiv Preussischer Kulturbesitz 18; Brooklyn Museum (49.48 Charles Edwin Wilbour Fund) 61; Cairo Museum 2, 32, 64-5, (photo Albert Shoucair) 22, 47, 56, 57, 58, 62, (photo Gallimard, l'Univers des Formes, Paris) 43 & 66 (photo Kodansha Ltd, Tokyo) 36; photo Peter Clayton 75; Ny Carlsberg Glyptothek, Copenhagen 38; photo André Held 42; Roemer-Pelizaeus Museum, Hildesheim 71; photo Max Hirmer 21; photo Kodansha Ltd, Tokyo 41, 45, 70; British Museum, London 1, 10-11, 13, 14, 15, 17, 19, 23, 30, 31, 51, 53, 54, 60, 63, 77; photo Kazimierz Michalowski 4-5, 28; Musée du Louvre, Paris, © Photo RMN 48; photo James Putnam 68-9; photo John Ross 34-5; photo Scala 25; photo Chris Scarre 72.
The quotations from *The Ancient Egyptian Book of the Dead* are taken from the translation by Raymond O. Faulkner, revised edition, published by British Museum Press.

© 1995 Thames & Hudson Ltd, London
Reprinted 2000

British Library Cataloguing-in-Publication Data
A catalogue record for this book is available from the British Library

ISBN 0-500-06013-4

Printed and bound in Slovenia by Mladinska Knjiga